Who Works Here?

Courthouse

by Lola M. Schaefer

Heinemann Library
Chicago, Illinois

© 2001 Reed Educational & Professional Publishing
Published by Heinemann Library,
an imprint of Reed Educational & Professional Publishing,
100 N. LaSalle, Suite 1010
Chicago, IL 60602
Customer Service 888-454-2279
Visit our website at www.heinemannlibrary.com

Designed by Wilkinson Design
Printed in Hong Kong

05 04 03 02 01
10 9 8 7 6 5 4 3 2 1

Library of Congress Cataloging-in-Publication Data
Schaefer, Lola M., 1950-
    Courthouse / by Lola M. Schaefer.
        p. cm. -- (Who works here?)
    Includes bibliographical references and index.
    ISBN 1-58810-124-X
    1. Courts--United States--Officials and employees--Juvenile literature. [1.
    Courts--Officials and employees. 2. Occupations.] I. Title.

    KF8770.Z9 S33 2001
                                                                00-058117

Acknowledgments
Photography by Phil Martin and Kimberly Saar.
Special thanks to the staff at Cook County Courthouse in Chicago, Illinois, and to workers everywhere who take pride in what they do.

Every effort has been made to contact copyright holders of any material reproduced in this book. Any omissions will be rectified in subsequent printings if notice is given to the publisher.

Some words are shown in bold, **like this.**
You can find out what they mean by looking in the glossary.

Contents

What Is a Courthouse?

Courthouses around the United States uphold the country's laws and the rights of its citizens.

A courthouse is a building where people work in the **justice** system. State attorneys **prosecute** people who have been arrested for crimes. These people, called **defendants,** hire **attorneys** or use the **public defender.** Both attorneys present **witnesses** and **evidence** to the court.

Judges and juries hear the **trial** cases in a courtroom. Afterward, they decide whether the defendants did the crimes. A large **staff** works together to follow the law and provide fair trials.

This is the Cook County Courthouse in Chicago, Illinois.
The map shows where the people in this book work.
Many courthouses in the United States look like this.

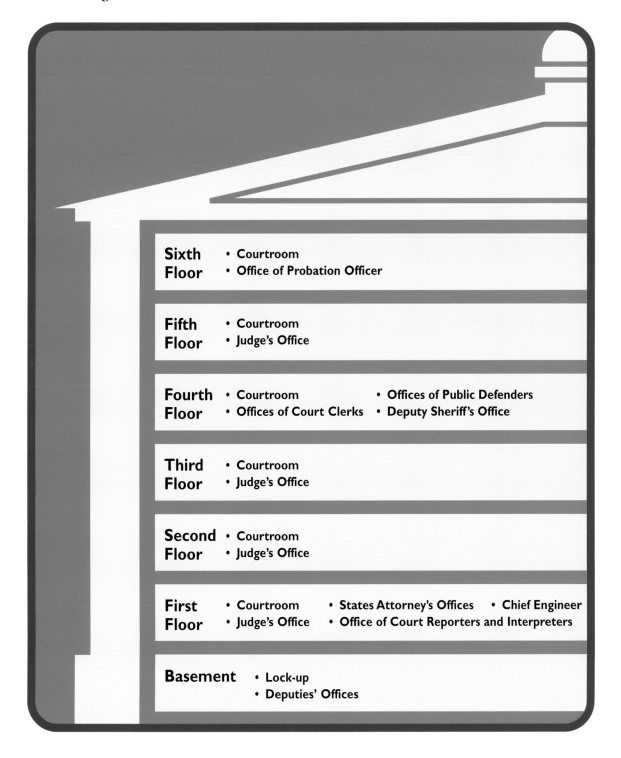

Sixth Floor
• Courtroom
• Office of Probation Officer

Fifth Floor
• Courtroom
• Judge's Office

Fourth Floor
• Courtroom
• Offices of Court Clerks
• Offices of Public Defenders
• Deputy Sheriff's Office

Third Floor
• Courtroom
• Judge's Office

Second Floor
• Courtroom
• Judge's Office

First Floor
• Courtroom
• Judge's Office
• States Attorney's Offices
• Office of Court Reporters and Interpreters
• Chief Engineer

Basement
• Lock-up
• Deputies' Offices

Judge

A judge is in charge of a courtroom during a **trial**. He or she decides when the **witnesses** can be heard and what **evidence** can be shown. If the **defendant** is found guilty of the crime, the judge gives the criminal a sentence he or she must serve.

This judge is listening to the state's **attorney** during a trial.

To become a judge, a man or woman has to go to college and law school. After passing a test called the bar exam, he or she can practice law. Most **attorneys** practice law for twelve or more years before becoming a judge. A judge can be voted into office or chosen by a higher court.

Here, the judge is putting on his robe before court.

Administrative Assistant

An administrative assistant keeps a judge's office neat. He or she schedules meetings for the judge and support **staff.** An administrative assistant copies and files court **documents** and helps the staff with each case.

Laurie is the administrative assistant in this office. She is speaking to a **defendant's** family about his case.

Laurie is helping the judge plan his meetings for the next week.

Most administrative assistants receive training while they work. Usually these people have held other jobs in the court system. They understand how the **justice** system works.

Deputy Sheriff

Tom is a deputy sheriff. Here, he is calling the court to order.

A deputy sheriff keeps the judge and all the people in the courtroom safe. He or she brings **inmates** from the **lockup** into the courtroom and **escorts** them in front of the judge. When the **trials** are over, the deputy sheriff takes the inmates back to the lockup.

Deputy sheriffs go to the Sheriff's Academy for ten weeks. They learn how to keep the courthouse safe. The deputy sheriff places **staff** at the front door. They check all visitors and their bags. They know how to stop and arrest anyone that is a danger to others.

Front-door security called this deputy sheriff to take a photographer to a judge's office.

Assistant State's Attorney

An assistant state's attorney **prosecutes** people who break the law. He or she comes to court in front of the judge and tries to settle the case with the defense **attorney**. If they cannot come to an agreement, the case goes to **trial**.

Isreal is an assistant state's attorney. Here, he is asking for background information on the **defendant.**

Isreal is reading the law to prepare for his next trial.

Assistant state's attorneys work with the police after someone is arrested. They search hard for all the facts before a trial. They review the **evidence** and interview **witnesses** about the crime. Isreal, like other assistant state's attorneys, wants **justice** for the **victims** and their families.

Assistant Public Defender

Melanie is an assistant public defender. She is asking a witness what she saw during a robbery.

Assistant public defenders **represent** people who cannot afford to pay an **attorney**. They explain the state's case to the **defendant**. They ask the defendant to explain all the events of the crime. Assistant public defenders find **witnesses** and present a good case for each of their **clients**.

Assistant public defenders had to go to college and law school. After they pass the bar exam, they can practice law. Assistant public defenders listen carefully to their clients. They prepare notes, **witnesses,** and **evidence** to support the defendant's case.

Here, Melanie reads the notes about the arrest and first **hearing** of the defendant she is representing.

Jury Supervisor

Allen, a jury supervisor, sends 40 jurors to a courtroom with a deputy sheriff.

A jury supervisor prepares people to serve on a jury. A jury is a group of people who live in the county where the courthouse is located. The people on the jury are called jurors. They receive a **summons** in the mail at their homes. When these people report for jury duty at the courthouse, the jury supervisor greets them and explains what a jury does during a **trial**.

A jury supervisor works well with his or her **staff**. Together, they record the time when each juror enters the jury room. They give out paychecks for the time that jurors spend away from their jobs.

Allen and a staff member study jury records to know how many summonses to send out for the next month.

Court Interpreter

A court interpreter **translates** languages in the courtroom. This person speaks another language other than English. A court interpreter helps **victims, defendants,** and **witnesses** understand what is being said by translating the English into another language.

Maribel is interpreting for a Spanish-speaking witness during a trial.

Most court interpreters attend two weeks of training in a classroom. They practice public speaking skills. They learn the different **legal** terms and how the justice system works. Afterward, court interpreters watch and practice in a courtroom for two more weeks.

A group of court interpreters meets in the office to talk about words that are hard to translate.

Court Reporter

The court reporter records everything that is said in the courtroom. He or she presses keys on a stenograph machine, which looks a little bit like a typewriter. The keys type **shorthand** symbols that stand for words. Later, the court reporter edits the notes and prints a written record of the **hearing**.

Pam is a court reporter. She is typing what this **witness** is saying during the **trial.**

A court reporter attends a school for court recording for three or more years. He or she must pass a state exam to become **certified** as a **shorthand** reporter. A court reporter must listen carefully to record the exact words said in court.

Pam is reading the shorthand record to the judge, because he asked to hear the **witness's** words again.

Court Clerk

A court clerk prepares court records for many people in the justice system. This person uses the computer to find information about the **defendant** and later puts that information into the case file. Court clerks answer questions about the court cases for the police department and the defendant's family

Toni, a court clerk, sits next to the judge and records all court activity.

Toni is also a court clerk trainer. Some people working in the clerk's office train with her for about three months to become a court clerk. They need strong writing, computer, and speaking skills. Court clerks work carefully when putting together the files for the different court cases.

Here, Toni is **swearing in** a **witness** in the courtroom.

Court Clerk Office Supervisor

The court clerk office supervisor helps his or her **staff** do their best work. He or she assigns clerks to the different courtrooms. The court clerk office supervisor and staff update the court computer system with the newest case information.

Rich is a court clerk office supervisor. Here, he helps a new clerk find case information for a **defendant's** family.

This court clerk office supervisor is helping a courtroom clerk work on the computer.

Most supervisors have worked in the different jobs in the court clerk's office, and they know the skills needed to do each job. The supervisor asks his or her staff to check all of their work. The information they share about the justice system must always be correct.

Probation Officer

A probation officer works with people after they receive a sentence of **probation** from the judge. A probation officer meets often with each **client**. He or she helps the clients with any special needs so they can obey the terms of the probation.

Tom is a probation officer. He is meeting a new client for the first time.

Here the probation officer is asking the client if
he has completed his **community service.**

Tom, like many other probation officers, went to a six-
week training class. Afterward, he worked with another
probation officer for two weeks. He learned what a
probation officer does in court, how to complete the
paperwork, and how to report to the court on each client.

Chief Engineer

George is a chief engineer. He is resetting
the fire alarms in the courthouse.

A chief engineer keeps all the **equipment** in the
courthouse working well. He or she trains a **staff** of
engineers and **mechanical** assistants. With the help of
these people, the chief engineer can answer calls or
work orders from the courthouse staff day and night.

Chief engineers go to **technical** school for 2-4 years. They learn all about building equipment and how it works. Later, they take classes to learn how to manage people on their staff. Chief engineers try to keep the courthouse comfortable for the staff.

Here, George and another engineer are checking to make sure the cooling system is working correctly.

Glossary

attorney lawyer

certified licensed to perform a job after passing a test proving knowledge of important information

client person or company that is being represented by a professional person, such as a lawyer; defendants are also clients

community service work done without pay that helps the community

defendant person in a court case who has been accused of a crime or who is being sued

document written record that is used to prove something

equipment tools and machines used for a special purpose

escort to accompany or protect someone

evidence information and facts that help prove something or make you believe that something is true

hearing the first time an accused person goes before the judge with testimony

inmate someone who has been sentenced, or is awaiting trial, who lives in a prison or other institution under supervision

justice fair and impartial behavior or treatment

legal having to do with the law

lockup jail, or holding room, in a courthouse where defendants are held before their court hearing or trial

manage to be in charge of people or a business

mechanical to do with machines or tools

probation period of time for testing a person's character or behavior, which is used instead of a more serious punishment

prosecute carry out a legal action in a court of law against a person accused of a crime

public defender lawyer who works for the state to defend people charged with a crime if they cannot pay for their own lawyer

represent speak or act for someone else

shorthand system of writing symbols instead of words; shorthand is used to take notes quickly

staff group of people who work for a company or person

summons an order to appear in court

swear in to make someone promise to tell the truth

technical to do with science or the mechanical arts

translate to express in a different language

trial act of hearing a case in court to decide whether a charge is true

victim someone who is hurt or treated badly

witness person who has seen or heard something

More Books to Read

Flanagan, Alice. Illustrated by Christine Osinski. *A Day in Court with Mrs. Trinh.* Danbury, Conn.: Children's Press, 1997.

An older reader can help you with these:

Kelly, Zachary A. *Judges and Lawyers.* Vero Beach, Fla.: Rourke Publications, Inc., 1998.

Kelly, Zachary A. *Our Court System.* Vero Beach, Fla.: Rourke Publications, Inc., 1998.

Index